Low-Fat Air Fryer Recipes

Low-Fat Mouthwatering Recipes on a Budget to Cook with Your Air Fryer for a Healthier Living

Linda Wang

© **Copyright 2021 by Linda Wang - All rights reserved.**

The content contained within this book may not be reproduced, duplicated or transmitted without direct written permission from the author or the publisher.
Under no circumstances will any blame or legal responsibility be held against the publisher, or author, for any damages, reparation, or monetary loss due to the information contained within this book. Either directly or indirectly.

Legal Notice:
This book is copyright protected. This book is only for personal use. You cannot amend, distribute, sell, use, quote or paraphrase any part, or the content within this book, without the consent of the author or publisher.

Disclaimer Notice:
Please note the information contained within this document is for educational and entertainment purposes only. All effort has been executed to present accurate, up to date, and reliable, complete information. No warranties of any kind are declared or implied. Readers acknowledge that the author is not engaging in the rendering of legal, financial, medical or professional advice. The content within this book has been derived from various sources. Please consult a licensed professional before attempting any techniques outlined in this book.
By reading this document, the reader agrees that under no circumstances is the author responsible for any losses, direct or indirect, which are incurred as a result of the use of information contained within this document, including, but not limited to, — errors, omissions, or inaccuracies.

TABLE OF CONTENTS

INTRODUCTION 1

Bell Pepper Eggs 5

Tex-Mex Hash Browns 7

Air Fryer Breakfast Casserole 9

Carrots and Cauliflower Mix 11

Bell Peppers Stew 13

Spinach and Shrimp 15

Turkey and Broccoli Stew 17

Fried Paprika Tofu 19

Easy Home Fries 20

Amazing Cheese Lings 22

Different Potatoes Gratin 23

Cheese and Spinach Balls 25

Special Walnut Stilton Circles 27

Lemon Chili Salmon 28

Parmesan Walnut Salmon 30

Cheesy Shrimp 32

Breaded Fried Shrimp 34

Baked Cod 36

Fried Salmon 38

Duck and Sauce 40

Cajun Chicken and Okra 42

Crunchy Chicken Strips 44

Popcorn Chicken 46

Chicken Fajita Rollups 48

Za'atar Lamb Loin Chops 50

Tomato Stuffed Pork Roll 52

Ham Rolls 54

Marinated Lamb and Veggies 56

Lamb Meatballs 58

Hot Pork Delight 60

Indian Turnips Salad 62

Green Beans and Lime Sauce 64

Stuffed Pumpkin 65

Jacket Potatoes 67

Stuffed Okra 69

Potato Soup 71

Garlic Soup with Almonds 74

Carrot Peanut Butter Soup 76

Vegetable spring rolls (Vegan) 78

Salsa Stuffed Eggplants (Vegan) 80

Zucchini Salsa 83

Bacon Filled Poppers 85

Spiced Avocado Pudding 87

Dried Raspberries 88

Chocolate Strawberry Cups 89

Air Fryer Chocolate Cake 90

Crème Brûlée 92

Zucchini-Choco Bread 94

Yummy Banana Cookies 97

Strawberry Muffins 99

NOTES 101

INTRODUCTION

An Air Fryer is a magic revolutionized kitchen appliance that helps you fry with less or even no oil at all. This kind of product applies Rapid Air technology, which offers a new way to fry with less oil. This new invention cooks food through the circulation of superheated air and generates 80% low-fat food. Although the food is fried with less oil, you don't need to worry as the food processed by the Air Fryer still has the same taste like the food fried using the deep-frying method.

This technology uses a superheated element, which radiates heat close to the food and an exhaust fan in its lid to circulate airflow. An Air Fryer ensures that the food processed is cooked completely. The exhaust fan located at the top of the cooking chamber helps the food get the same heating temperature in every part quickly, resulting in a cooked food of better and healthier quality. Besides, cooking with an Air Fryer is also suitable for those individuals which are too busy or do not have enough time. For example, an Air Fryer only needs half a spoonful of oil and takes 10 minutes to serve a medium bowl of crispy French fries.

In addition to serving healthier food, an Air Fryer also provides some other benefits to you. Since an Air Fryer helps you fry using less oil or without oil for some kind of food, it automatically reduces the fat and cholesterol content in food. Indeed, no one will refuse to enjoy fried food without worrying about the greasy and fat content. Having fried food with no guilt is one of the pleasures of life. Besides having low fat and cholesterol, you save some amount of money by consuming oil sparingly, which can be used for other needs. An Air Fryer also can reheat your food. Sometimes, when you have fried leftover and you reheat it, it will usually serve reheated greasy food with some addition of unhealthy reuse oil. Undoubtedly, the saturated fat in the fried food gets worse because of this process. An Air Fryer helps you reheat your food without being afraid of extra oils that the food may absorb. Fried bananas, fish and chips, nuggets, or even fried chicken can be reheated to become as warm and crispy as they were before by using an Air Fryer.

Some people may think that spending some amount of money to buy a fryer is wasteful. I dare to say that they are wrong because an Air Fryer is not only used to fry. It is a sophisticated multi-function appliance since it also helps you to roast chicken, make steak, grill fish, and even bake a cake. With a built-in air filter, an Air Fryer filters the air and saves your kitchen from smoke and grease.

An air Fryer is really a new innovative method of cooking. Grab it fast and welcome to a clean and healthy kitchen.

Bell Pepper Eggs

Preparation Time: 25 minutes

Servings: 4

Ingredients:

- 3 oz. cooked ham; chopped
- 4 medium green bell peppers
- ¼ medium onion; peeled and chopped

- 8 large eggs.
- 1 cup mild Cheddar cheese

Directions:

1. Cut the tops off each bell pepper. Remove the seeds and the white membranes with a small knife. Place ham and onion into each pepper
2. Crack 2 eggs into each pepper. Top with ¼ cup cheese per pepper. Place into the air fryer basket
3. Adjust the temperature to 390 Degrees F and set the timer for 15 minutes. When fully cooked, peppers will be tender and eggs will be firm. Serve immediately.

Nutrition:

Calories: 314; Protein: 24.9g; Fiber: 1.7g; Fat: 18.6g; Carbs: 6.3g

Tex-Mex Hash Browns

Preparation Time: 15 minutes

Cooking Time: 30 minutes

Servings: 4

Ingredients:

- 1½ pounds potatoes, peeled, cut into 1-inch cubes and soaked
- 1 small onion, cut into 1-inch pieces
- 1 red bell pepper, seeded and cut into 1-inch pieces
- 1 jalapeno, seeded and cut into 1-inch rings
- 1 tablespoon olive oil
- ½ teaspoon taco seasoning mix
- ½ teaspoon ground cumin
- 1 pinch salt and ground black pepper, to taste

Directions:

1. Preheat the Air fryer to 330 degrees F and grease an Air fryer basket.

2. Coat the potatoes with olive oil and transfer into the Air fryer basket.
3. Cook for about 18 minutes and dish out in a bowl.
4. Mix together bell pepper, onion, and jalapeno in the bowl and season with the taco seasoning mix, cumin, salt and black pepper.
5. Toss to coat well and combine with the potatoes.
6. Transfer the seasoned vegetables into the Air fryer basket and cook for about 12 minutes, stirring in between.
7. Dish out and serve immediately.

Nutrition:

Calories: 186, Fat: 4.3g, Carbohydrates: 33.7g, Sugar: 3g, Protein: 4g, Sodium: 79mg

Air Fryer Breakfast Casserole

Preparation Time: 10 minutes

Cooking Time: 25 minutes

Servings: 2

Ingredients:

- 3 eggs
- 3 red potatoes
- 2 turkey sausage patties
- ¼ cup cheddar cheese
- 1 tablespoon milk
- Olive oil cooking spray

Directions:

1. Preheat the Air fryer to 400 °F and grease a baking dish with cooking spray.
2. Place the potatoes in the Air fryer basket and cook for about 10 minutes.
3. Whisk eggs with milk in a bowl.

4. Put the potatoes and sausage in the baking dish and pour egg mixture on top.
5. Sprinkle with cheddar cheese and arrange in the Air fryer.
6. Cook for about 15 minutes at 350 °F and dish out to serve warm.

Nutrition:

Calories: 469, Fat: 16.3g, Carbohydrates: 51.9g, Sugar: 4.1g, Protein: 29.1g, Sodium: 623mg

Carrots and Cauliflower Mix

Preparation Time: 30 minutes

Servings: 4

Ingredients:

- 1 cauliflower head; stems removed, florets separated and steamed
- 2 oz. cheddar cheese; grated
- 2 oz. milk

- 3 eggs
- 3 carrots; chopped and steamed
- 2 tsp. cilantro; chopped.
- Salt and black pepper to taste

Directions:

1. In a bowl, mix the eggs with the milk, parsley, salt and pepper; whisk. Put the cauliflower and the carrots in your air fryer, add the egg mixture and spread. Then sprinkle the cheese on top
2. Cook at 350 °F for 20 minutes, divide between plates and serve

Bell Peppers Stew

Preparation Time: 20 minutes

Servings: 4

Ingredients:

- 2 yellow bell peppers; cut into wedges
- 2 red bell peppers; cut into wedges
- ½ cup tomato sauce

- 2 green bell peppers; cut into wedges
- ¼ tsp. sweet paprika
- 1 tbsp. chili powder
- 2 tsp. cumin, ground
- Salt and black pepper to taste.

Directions:

1. In a pan that fits your air fryer, mix all the ingredients, toss, introduce the pan in the machine and cook at 370 °F for 15 minutes
2. Divide into bowls.

Nutrition:

Calories: 190; Fat: 4g; Fiber: 2g; Carbs: 4g; Protein: 7g

Spinach and Shrimp

Preparation Time: 20 minutes

Servings: 4

Ingredients:

- 15 oz. shrimp; peeled and deveined
- 2 tomatoes; cubed
- ¼ cup veggie stock

- 4 spring onions; chopped.
- 2 cups baby spinach
- 2 tbsp. cilantro; chopped.
- 1 tbsp. garlic; minced
- 1 tbsp. lemon juice
- ½ tsp. cumin, ground
- Salt and black pepper to taste.

Directions:

1. In a pan that fits your air fryer, mix all the ingredients except the cilantro, toss, introduce in the air fryer and cook at 360 °F for 15 minutes
2. Add the cilantro, stir, divide into bowls.

Nutrition:

Calories: 201; Fat: 8g; Fiber: 2g; Carbs: 4g; Protein: 8g

Turkey and Broccoli Stew

Preparation Time: 30 minutes

Servings: 4

Ingredients:

- 1 broccoli head, florets separated
- 1 turkey breast, skinless; boneless and cubed
- 1 tbsp. parsley; chopped.
- 1 cup tomato sauce

- 1 tbsp. olive oil
- Salt and black pepper to taste.

Directions:

1. In a baking dish that fits your air fryer, mix the turkey with the rest of the ingredients except the parsley, toss, introduce the dish in the fryer, bake at 380 °F for 25 minutes
2. Divide into bowls, sprinkle the parsley on top and serve.

Nutrition:

Calories: 250; Fat: 11g; Fiber: 2g; Carbs: 6g; Protein: 12g

Fried Paprika Tofu

Preparation Time: 25 minutes

Servings: 2

Ingredients:

- 1 block extra firm tofu; pressed to remove excess water and cut into cubes
- 1/4 cup cornstarch
- salt and pepper to taste
- 1 tablespoon smoked paprika

Directions:

1. Line the Air Fryer basket with aluminum foil and brush with oil. Preheat the Air Fryer to 370 - degrees Fahrenheit.
2. Mix all ingredients in a bowl. Toss to combine. Place in the Air Fryer basket and cook for 12 minutes.

Easy Home Fries

Preparation Time: 20 minutes

Servings: 4

Ingredients:

- 1 medium green bell pepper; seeded and diced
- ½ medium white onion; peeled and diced
- 1 medium jicama; peeled.

- 1 tbsp. coconut oil; melted
- ½ tsp. pink Himalayan salt
- ¼ tsp. ground black pepper

Directions:

1. Cut jicama into 1-inch cubes. Place into a large bowl and toss with coconut oil until coated. Sprinkle with pepper and salt. Place into the air fryer basket with peppers and onion.
2. Adjust the temperature to 400 Degrees F and set the timer for 10 minutes. Shake two or three times during cooking. Jicama will be tender and dark around edges. Serve immediately.

Nutrition:

Calories: 97; Protein: 1.5g; Fiber: 8.0g; Fat: 3.3g; Carbs: 15.8g

Amazing Cheese Lings

Preparation Time: 25 minutes

Servings: 2

Ingredients:
- 1 cup flour [all-purpose]
- 3 small cubes cheese [grated]
- 1 teaspoon butter
- 1/4 teaspoon chili powder
- salt to taste
- 1 teaspoon baking powder

Directions:
1. Make dough with all the ingredients mentioned above and add small amount water if needed.
2. Roll and cut the pieces into round shape.
3. Preheat Air Fryer to 360 - degrees Fahrenheit and air fry for 5 minutes. Stir halfway and periodically.

Different Potatoes Gratin

Preparation Time: 55 minutes

Servings: 4

Ingredients:

- 1/2 cup milk
- 1/2 cup cream
- 7 medium russet potatoes; peeled
- 1 teaspoon black pepper
- 1/2 cup semi-mature cheese; grated
- 1/2 teaspoon nutmeg

Directions:

1. Preheat the Air Fryer to 390 – degrees Fahrenheit.
2. Slice the potatoes wafer-thin. In a bowl; mix the milk and cream and season to taste with salt, pepper, and nutmeg.
3. Coat the potato slices with this mixture. Transfer the potato slices to an 8-inch heat-resistant baking dish. Pour the rest of the cream mixture

on top of the potatoes.

4. In the cooking basket of the Air Fryer; place the baking dish and set the timer to 25 minutes.
5. Remove cooking basket and distribute the cheese evenly over the potatoes. Set the timer for 10 minutes and bake the gratin until it is nicely browned.

Cheese and Spinach Balls

Preparation Time: 35 minutes

Servings: 3

Ingredients:

- 1 cup spinach [boiled]
- 1 cup corn flour
- 2 onion [chopped]
- 1 cup bread crumbs

- 1 tablespoon red chili flakes
- 1/2 cup mozzarella [grated]
- 1 teaspoon garlic [grated]
- 1 tablespoon salt
- 2 tablespoon olive oil

Directions:

1. Mix all ingredients and form the mixture into small balls. Brush the pan with oil.
2. Air fry at 390 - degrees Fahrenheit for 15 minutes. Serve them with tartar sauce.

Special Walnut Stilton Circles

Preparation Time: 45 minutes

Servings: 2

Ingredients:

- 1/4 cup flour [plain]
- 1/4 cup walnuts
- 1/4 cup butter
- 1/4 cup stilton

Directions:

1. Make dough with all the ingredients mentioned above by mixing them well till a thick texture appears. Cut dough into log shapes, approx. 3cm.
2. Wrap it in aluminum foil and let it freeze for about 30 minutes. Now cut the dough into circles.
3. Line Air Fryer with baking sheet and preheat to 350 - degrees Fahrenheit. Cook 20 minutes. And it is ready! Serve while its hot.

Lemon Chili Salmon

Preparation Time: 10 minutes

Cooking Time: 17 minutes

Serve: 4

Ingredients:

- 2 lbs salmon fillet, skinless and boneless
- 1 orange juice

- 1 tbsp olive oil
- 2 lemon juice
- 1 bunch fresh dill
- 1 chili, sliced
- Pepper
- Salt

Directions:

1. Preheat the air fryer to 325 °F.
2. Place salmon fillets in air fryer baking pan and drizzle with olive oil, lemon juice, and orange juice.
3. Sprinkle chili slices over salmon and season with pepper and salt.
4. Place pan in the air fryer and cook for 15-17 minutes.
5. Garnish with dill and serve.

Nutrition:

Calories 339, Fat 17.5 g, Carbohydrates 2 g, Sugar 2 g, Protein 44 g, Cholesterol 100 mg

Parmesan Walnut Salmon

Preparation Time: 10 minutes

Cooking Time: 12 minutes

Serve: 4

Ingredients:

- 4 salmon fillets
- 1/4 cup parmesan cheese, grated
- 1 tsp olive oil
- 1/2 cup walnuts
- 1 tbsp lemon rind

Directions:

1. Preheat the air fryer to 370 °F.
2. Spray an air fryer baking dish with cooking spray.
3. Place salmon on a baking dish.
4. Add walnuts into the food processor and process until finely ground.

5. Mix ground walnuts with parmesan cheese, oil, and lemon rind. Stir well.
6. Spoon walnut mixture over the salmon and press gently.
7. Place in the air fryer and cook for 12 minutes.
8. Serve and enjoy.

Nutrition:

Calories 420, Fat 27.4 g, Carbohydrates 2 g, Sugar 0.3 g, Protein 46.3 g, Cholesterol 98 mg

Cheesy Shrimp

Preparation Time: 20 minutes

Cooking Time: 20 minutes

Servings: 4

Ingredients:

- 2/3 cup Parmesan cheese, grated
- 2 pounds shrimp, peeled and deveined
- 2 tablespoons olive oil
- 4 garlic cloves, minced
- 1 teaspoon dried basil
- ½ teaspoon dried oregano
- 1 teaspoon onion powder
- ½ teaspoon red pepper flakes, crushed
- Ground black pepper, as required
- 2 tablespoons fresh lemon juice

Directions:

1. Preheat the Air fryer to 350 degrees F and grease an Air fryer basket.

2. Mix Parmesan cheese, garlic, olive oil, herbs, and spices in a large bowl.
3. Arrange half of the shrimp into the Air fryer basket in a single layer and cook for about 10 minutes.
4. Dish out the shrimps onto serving plates and drizzle with lemon juice to serve hot.

Nutrition:

Calories: 386, Fat: 14.2g, Carbohydrates: 5.3g, Sugar: 0.4g, Protein: 57.3g, Sodium: 670mg

Breaded Fried Shrimp

Preparation time: 10 minutes

Servings: 4

Ingredients:

- Raw shrimp: 1 lb.
- Egg white: 3 tbsp. or 1 egg
- All-purpose flour: .5 cup
- Panko breadcrumbs: .75 cup
- Pepper & salt: as desired
- McCormick's Grill Mates Montreal Chicken Seasoning
- Paprika: 1 tsp.
- Cooking oil spray: as needed

Ingredients - The Sauce:

- Sriracha: 2 tbsp.
- Plain non-fat Greek yogurt: .33 cup
- Sweet chili sauce: .25 cup

Directions:
1. Peel and devein the shrimp.
2. Set the temperature of the Air Fryer to 400º Fahrenheit.
3. Add the seasonings to the shrimp.
4. Use three bowls for the breadcrumbs, egg whites, and flour.
5. Dip the shrimp into the flour, the egg, and the breadcrumbs.
6. Lightly spritz the shrimp with the cooking spray and add to the fryer basket for four minutes.
7. Flip the shrimp and continue cooking for another four minutes.
8. Combine all of the fixings for the sauce and toss with the shrimp before serving.

Baked Cod

Preparation Time: 18 minutes

Servings: 4

Ingredients:

- 4 cod fillets; boneless
- 1/2 tsp. oregano; dried
- 3/4 tsp. sweet paprika

- 2 tbsp. parsley; chopped.
- 1/2 tsp. thyme; dried
- 1/2 tsp. basil; dried
- 2 tbsp. butter; melted
- A drizzle of olive oil
- Juice of 1 lemon
- Salt and black pepper to taste

Directions:

1. Add all ingredients to a bowl and toss gently.
2. Transfer the fish to your air fryer and cook at 380 °F for 6 minutes on each side. Serve right away

Fried Salmon

Preparation Time: 22 minutes

Servings: 4

Ingredients:

- 4 salmon fillets; boneless
- 1 white onion; chopped.
- 3 tbsp. olive oil

- 3 tomatoes; sliced
- 4 cilantro sprigs; chopped.
- 4 thyme sprigs; chopped.
- 1 lemon; sliced
- Salt and black pepper to taste

Directions:

1. In your air fryer, mix the salmon with the oil, onions, tomatoes, thyme, cilantro, salt and pepper
2. Top with the lemon slices and cook at 360 °F for 12 minutes. Divide everything between plates and serve.

Duck and Sauce

Preparation Time: 30 minutes

Servings: 4

Ingredients:

- 2 duck breasts; skin scored
- 1 tbsp. garlic; minced
- 8 oz. white wine

- 2 tbsp. heavy cream
- 2 tbsp. cranberries
- 1 tbsp. sugar
- 1 tbsp. olive oil
- Salt and black pepper to taste

Directions:

1. Season the duck breasts with salt and pepper and put them in the preheated air fryer
2. Cook at 350 °F for 10 minutes on each side and divide between plates
3. Heat up a pan with the oil over medium heat and add the cranberries, sugar, wine, garlic and the cream; whisk well. Cook for 3-4 minutes, drizzle over the duck and serve.

Cajun Chicken and Okra

Preparation Time: 40 minutes

Servings: 4

Ingredients:

- 1 lb. chicken thighs; halved
- 1/2 lb. okra
- 1 yellow onion; chopped.
- 1 red bell pepper; chopped.

- 1 cup chicken stock
- 1 tbsp. Cajun spice
- 4 garlic cloves; minced
- 1 tbsp. olive oil
- Salt and black pepper to taste

Directions:

1. Add the oil to a pan that fits your air fryer and heat up over medium heat.
2. Then add the chicken and brown for 2-3 minutes
3. Next, add all remaining ingredients, toss and cook for 3-4 minutes more
4. Place the pan into the air fryer and cook at 380°F for 22 minutes. Divide everything between plates and serve.

Crunchy Chicken Strips

Cooking Time: 12 minutes

Servings: 8

Ingredients:

- 1 chicken breast; cut into strips
- 1/4 cup almond flour
- 3/4 cup breadcrumbs

- 1 egg; beaten
- 1 tsp. mix spice
- 1 tbsp. plain oats
- 1 tbsp. dried coconut
- Salt and pepper to taste

Directions:

1. In a bowl, mix oats, mix spice, coconut, pepper, salt and breadcrumbs. Add beaten egg to another bowl. Add the flour to a third dish
2. Take the flour and coat chicken strips with it, then dip in egg and roll in breadcrumb mixture. Place the coated chicken strips in air fryer basket and air fry at 350 °F and cook for 4 minutes. Serve hot!

Popcorn Chicken

Cooking Time: 10 minutes

Servings: 12

Ingredients:

- 1 chicken breast; boneless
- 1/4 cup almond flour
- 1 cup breadcrumbs

- 2 tsp. mix spice
- 1 egg; beaten
- Salt and pepper to taste

Directions:

1. Add the chicken to your food processor and process it until it is minced. In a bowl, add the beaten egg. In another bowl, add the flour
2. In a third shallow dish add the breadcrumbs, mix spice, pepper and salt and stir to combine. Make small chicken balls from minced chicken.
3. Roll chicken balls in flour, then dip into egg, then coat with breadcrumbs. Place coated chicken balls into air fryer and air fry at 350 °F for 10 minutes. Serve hot!

Chicken Fajita Rollups

Cooking Time: 12 minutes

Servings: 6

Ingredients:

- 3 chicken breasts
- 1/2 large yellow bell pepper; cut into strips
- 1/2 large red onion; sliced
- 1/2 large red bell pepper; cut into strips
- 1/2 large green bell pepper; cut into strips
- 2 tsp. paprika
- 1 tsp. cumin powder
- 1 tsp. garlic powder
- 1/2 tsp. cayenne pepper
- 1/2 tsp. Mexican oregano
- Cooking spray
- Salt and pepper; to taste

Directions:

1. Mix spices in a small bowl and set aside. Slice the chicken breasts lengthwise into 2 even slices.
2. Then, place each breast half between parchment paper and firmly pound it using a heavy object to an even thickness of ¼ of an inch
3. Liberally season both sides of the breast with the prepared spice rub
4. Afterwards, portion the vegetable strips evenly among the cuts and place each portion on one side of the chicken. Roll up the chicken tightly and secure with toothpicks. Sprinkle the remaining spice rub
5. Mist the air fryer basket with cooking spray and place the rollups in it. Spray the chicken with more cooking spray, then air fry for 12 minutes. Repeat until all the rollups are cooked, then serve

Za'atar Lamb Loin Chops

Preparation Time: 10 minutes

Cooking Time: 30 minutes

Servings: 4

Ingredients:

- 3 garlic cloves, crushed
- 8: 3½-ouncesbone-in lamb loin chops, trimmed
- 1 tablespoon fresh lemon juice
- 1 teaspoon olive oil
- 1 tablespoon Za'ataro
- Salt and black pepper, to taste

Directions:

1. Preheat the Air fryer to 400 degrees F and grease an Air fryer basket.
2. Mix the garlic, lemon juice, oil, Za'atar, salt, and black pepper in a large bowl.
3. Coat the chops generously with the herb mixture and arrange the chops in the Air fryer basket.

4. Cook for about 15 minutes, flipping twice in between and dish out the lamb chops to serve hot.

Nutrition:

Calories: 433, Fat: 17.6g, Carbohydrates: 0.6g, Sugar: 0.2g, Protein: 64.1g, Sodium: 201mg

(Note: Za'atar - Za'atar is generally made with ground dried thyme, oregano, marjoram, or some combination thereof, mixed with toasted sesame seeds, and salt, though other spices such as sumac might also be added. Some commercial varieties also include roasted flour.

Tomato Stuffed Pork Roll

Preparation Time: 20 minutes

Cooking Time: 15 minutes

Servings: 4

Ingredients:

- 1 scallion, chopped
- ¼ cup sun-dried tomatoes, chopped finely
- 4: 6-ouncepork cutlets, pounded slightly
- 2 teaspoons paprika
- 2 tablespoons fresh parsley, chopped
- Salt and freshly ground black pepper, to taste
- ½ tablespoon olive oil

Directions:

1. Preheat the Air fryer to 390 degrees F and grease an Air fryer basket.
2. Mix scallion, tomatoes, parsley, salt and black pepper in a bowl.

3. Coat each cutlet with tomato mixture and roll up the cutlet, securing with cocktail sticks.
4. Coat the rolls with oil and rub with paprika, salt and black pepper.
5. Arrange the rolls in the Air fryer basket and cook for about 15 minutes, flipping once in between.
6. Dish out in a platter and serve warm.

Nutrition:

Calories: 244, Fat: 14.5g, Carbohydrates: 20.1g, Sugar: 1.7g, Protein: 8.2g, Sodium: 670mg

Ham Rolls

Preparation Time: 15 minutes

Cooking Time: 15 minutes

Servings: 4

Ingredients:

- 1/3 pound cooked ham, sliced
- 12-ounce refrigerated pizza crust, rolled into ¼ inch thickness
- ¾ cup Mozzarella cheese, shredded
- 3 cups Colby cheese, shredded
- 3-ounce roasted red bell peppers
- 1 tablespoon olive oil

Directions:

1. Preheat the Air fryer to 360 degrees F and grease an Air fryer basket.
2. Arrange the ham, cheeses and roasted peppers over one side of the dough and fold to seal.
3. Brush the dough evenly with olive oil and cook for about 15 minutes, flipping twice in between.
4. Dish out in a platter and serve warm.

Nutrition:

Calories: 594, Fat: 35.8g, Carbohydrates: 35.4g, Sugar: 2.8g, Protein: 33g, Sodium: 1545mg

Marinated Lamb and Veggies

Preparation Time: 40 Minutes

Servings: 4

Ingredients:
- 1 carrot; chopped
- 1 onion; sliced
- 8-ounce lamb loin; sliced
- 1/2 tbsp. olive oil
- 3-ounce bean sprouts
- For the marinade:
- 1 garlic clove; minced
- 1/2 apple; grated
- 2 tbsp. orange juice
- 1 tbsp. sugar
- 5 tbsp. soy sauce
- 1 tbsp. ginger; grated
- 1 small yellow onion; grated
- Salt and black pepper to the taste

Directions:

1. In a bowl; mix 1 grated onion with the apple, garlic, 1 tablespoon ginger, soy sauce, orange juice, sugar and black pepper, whisk well, add lamb and leave aside for 10 minutes
2. Heat up a pan that fits your air fryer with the olive oil over medium high heat, add 1 sliced onion, carrot and bean sprouts; stir and cook for 3 minutes.
3. Add lamb and the marinade, transfer pan to your preheated air fryer and cook at 360°F, for 25 minutes. Divide everything into bowls and serve

Lamb Meatballs

Preparation Time: 22 minutes

Servings: 8

Ingredients:

- 4 oz. lamb meat; minced
- 1 tbsp. oregano; chopped.
- 1/2 tbsp. lemon zest
- 1 egg; whisked
- Salt and black pepper to taste
- Cooking spray

Directions:

1. In a bowl, combine all of the ingredients except the cooking spray and stir well.
2. Shape medium-sized meatballs out of this mix
3. Place the meatballs in your air fryer's basket, grease them with cooking spray and cook at 400°F for 12 minutes. Divide between plates and serve

Hot Pork Delight

Preparation Time: 28 minutes

Servings: 4

Ingredients:

- 1 lb. pork tenderloin; cubed
- 2 tbsp. olive oil
- 1 red onion; chopped.

- 3 tbsp. parsley; chopped.
- 1/2 tsp. hot chili powder
- 1 garlic clove; minced
- 1 tsp. cinnamon powder
- Salt and black pepper to taste

Directions:

1. In a bowl, combine the chili, cinnamon, garlic, salt, pepper and the oil. Then add the pork and rub it well with the mixture
2. Transfer the meat to your air fryer and cook at 280°F for 12 minutes. Add the onions and cook for 5 minutes more
3. Divide everything between plates and serve with the parsley sprinkled on top.

Indian Turnips Salad

Preparation Time: 10 minutes

Cooking time: 12 minutes

Servings: 4

Ingredients:

- 20 ounces turnips, peeled and chopped
- 1 teaspoon garlic, minced
- 2 yellow onions, chopped
- 1 teaspoon ginger, grated
- 2 tomatoes, chopped
- 1 teaspoon cumin, ground
- 1 teaspoon coriander, ground
- 2 green chilies, chopped
- ½ teaspoon turmeric powder
- 2 tablespoons butter
- Salt and black pepper to the taste
- A handful coriander leaves, chopped

Directions:

1. Heat up a pan that fits your air fryer with the butter, melt it, add green chilies, garlic and ginger, stir and cook for 1 minute.
2. Add onions, salt, pepper, tomatoes, turmeric, cumin, ground coriander and turnips, stir, introduce in your air fryer and cook at 350 °F for 10 minutes.
3. Divide among plates, sprinkle fresh coriander on top and serve.

Nutrition:

Calories: 163; Fat: 5g; Fiber: 2g; Carbs: 4g; Protein: 8g

Green Beans and Lime Sauce

Preparation Time: 13 minutes

Servings: 4

Ingredients:

- 1 lb. green beans, trimmed
- 1 tsp. chili powder
- 2 tbsp. ghee; melted
- 1 tbsp. lime juice
- A pinch of salt and black pepper

Directions:

1. Take a bowl and mix the ghee with the rest of the ingredients except the green beans and whisk really well.
2. Mix the green beans with the lime sauce, toss
3. Put them in your air fryer's basket and cook at 400 °F for 8 minutes. Serve right away.

Nutrition:

Calories: 151; Fat: 4g; Fiber: 2g; Carbs: 4g; Protein: 6g

Stuffed Pumpkin

Preparation Time: 20 minutes

Cooking Time: 35 minutes

Servings: 4

Ingredients:

- 1 bell pepper, chopped
- 2 tomatoes, chopped

- 1 beetroot, chopped
- 2 garlic cloves, minced
- ½ cup green beans, shelled
- ½ of butternut pumpkin, seeded
- 2 teaspoons mixed dried herbs
- Salt and black pepper, to taste

Directions:

1. Preheat the Air fryer to 360 degrees F and grease an Air fryer basket.
2. Mix all the ingredients in a bowl except pumpkin and toss to coat well.
3. Stuff the vegetable mixture into the pumpkin and place into the Air fryer basket.
4. Cook for about 35 minutes and keep aside to slightly cool.
5. Dish out and serve warm.

Nutrition:

Calories: 48, Fats: 0.4g, Carbohydrates: 11.1g, Sugar: 5.7g, Proteins: 1.8g, Sodium: 25mg

Jacket Potatoes

Preparation Time: 30 minutes

Servings: 2

Ingredients:

- 2 potatoes
- 1 tbsp. butter; softened
- 3 tbsp. sour cream

- 1 tbsp. mozzarella cheese, shredded
- 1 tsp. chives, minced
- Salt and ground black pepper; as your liking

Directions:

1. Set the temperature of air fryer to 355 °F. Grease an air fryer basket.
2. With a fork, prick the potatoes. Arrange potatoes into the prepared air fryer basket.
3. Air fry for about 15 minutes. In a bowl; add the remaining Ingredients and mix until well combined.
4. Remove from air fryer and transfer the potatoes onto a platter.
5. Open potatoes from the center and stuff them with cheese mixture. Serve immediately

Stuffed Okra

Preparation Time: 27 minutes

Servings: 2

Ingredients:

- 8-oz large okra
- 1/4 of onion; chopped
- 1/4 cup chickpea flour
- 2 tbsp. coconut; grated freshly
- 1 tsp. garam masala powder
- 1/2 tsp. ground turmeric
- 1/2 tsp. red chili powder
- 1/2 tsp. ground cumin
- Salt, to taste

Directions:

1. With a knife, make a slit in each okra vertically without cutting in 2 halves. In a bowl; mix together the flour, onion; grated coconut and spices.

2. Stuff each okra with the mixture. Set the temperature of air fryer to 390 °F. Grease an air fryer basket.
3. Arrange stuffed okra into the prepared air fryer basket. Air fry for about 12 minutes.
4. Remove from air fryer and transfer the okra onto serving plates. Serve hot.

Potato Soup

Preparation Time: 5 minutes

Cooking Time: 30 minutes

Servings: 5

Ingredients:

- 6 medium peeled and diced potatoes
- ¾ Cup of sliced baby carrots
- ½ Cup of fresh and chopped baby spinach leaves
- ½ Can of Progresso Creamy Garlic
- ½ Cup of chopped celery
- 1 Cup of chopped onion
- 1/8 Teaspoon of paprika
- 1 Cup of broth
- 1/8 Teaspoon of crushed red pepper
- 1 Tbsp of ground flax or you can use chia seeds
- ½ Teaspoon of salt
- Sharp grated cheddar cheese
- Basil leaves

Directions:

1. Place all of your ingredients inside your Air fryer and mix them very well.
2. Lock the led and set the button to Soup and set your timer to 30 minutes.

3. Once done, place a towel on the lid and try a fast pressure release; then insert your blender to immerse and keep repeating the same procedure until your soup become thick.
4. Taste your soup and add a pinch of salt if needed.
5. Serve your soup and enjoy it with Serve whole grain wheat bread.

Nutrition:

Calories – 208 Protein – 8.3 g. Fat – 6.1 g. Carbs – 28 g.

Garlic Soup with Almonds

Preparation Time: 5 minutes

Cooking Time: 15 minutes

Servings: 3

Ingredients:

- 3 and ¼ cups of freezing water
- 2 and ¼ cups of blanched almonds
- 5 Peeled and minced cloves of garlic
- ½ Cup of coconuts oil
- 1 Baguette (remove the crusts removed and cut it into pieces)
- 2 And ½ tbsp of sherry vinegar
- 2 Drops of almond extract
- 1 Pinch of Kosher salt

Directions:

1. Start by combining the 2 cups of water in the Instant Processor with the almonds, the garlic, and the bread in the food processor.

2. Set the manual to the button Sauté; sauté the ingredients soften for around 5 minutes.
3. Add the remaining quantity of water, the coconut oil, the vinegar, the extract, and the salt.
4. Cancel the setting of the Sauté feature and set the timer to 10 minutes
5. Once the timer is off, release the pressure and blend the ingredients with the a food processor or blender
6. Garnish your soup with the halves of almonds.
7. Serve and enjoy your soup!

Nutrition:

Calories – 120 Protein – 7.1 g. Fat – 13.4 g. Carbs – 37.1 g.

Carrot Peanut Butter Soup

Preparation Time: 5 minutes

Cooking Time: 15 minutes

Servings: 4

Ingredients:

- 8 carrots, peeled and chopped
- 1 onion, chopped
- 3 garlic cloves, peeled
- 14 oz. coconut milk
- ¼ cup peanut butter
- 1 ½ cup chicken stock
- 1 tbsp. curry paste
- Pepper
- Salt

Directions:

1. Add all ingredients except salt and pepper into air fryer and stir well.

2. Secure pot with lid and cook on manual high pressure for 15 minutes.
3. Quick release pressure then open the lid.
4. Puree the soup using an immersion blender until smooth.
5. Season soup with pepper and salt.
6. Serve and enjoy.

Nutrition:

Calories – 416 Protein – 8.2 g. Fat – 34.2 g. Carbs – 25.3 g.

Vegetable spring rolls (Vegan)

Preparation time: 15 minutes

Servings: 4

Ingredients

- ½ cabbage, grated
- 1 tsp minced ginger
- 2 carrots, grated

- 1 tsp minced garlic
- 1 tsp sesame oil
- 1 tsp sesame seeds
- 1 tsp soy sauce
- ½ tsp salt
- 1 tsp olive oil
- 1 package spring roll wrappers

Directions

1. Combine all ingredients in a large bowl.
2. Divide the mixture between the spring roll sheets and roll them up; arrange on the baking tray.
3. Cook in the oven for 5 minutes on bake at 370 degrees F.

Nutrition:

Calories: 65, Protein: 1.35g, Fat: 3.1g, Carbs: 8.28g

Salsa Stuffed Eggplants (Vegan)

Servings: 2

Preparation Time: 15 minutes

Cooking Time: 25 minutes

Ingredients

- 1 large eggplant
- 2 teaspoons olive oil, divided

- 8 cherry tomatoes, quartered
- 2 teaspoons fresh lemon juice, divided
- 2 tablespoons tomato salsa
- ½ tablespoon fresh parsley
- Salt and ground black pepper, as required

Directions:
1. Set the temperature of air fryer to 390 degrees F. Grease an air fryer basket.
2. Place eggplant into the prepared air fryer basket.
3. Air fry for about 15 minutes.
4. Remove from air fryer and cut the eggplant in half lengthwise.
5. Drizzle the eggplant halves evenly with one teaspoon of oil.
6. Now, set the temperature of air fryer to 355 degrees F. Grease the air fryer basket.
7. Arrange eggplant into the prepared air fryer basket, cut-side up.
8. Air fry for another 10 minutes.

9. Remove eggplant from the air fryer and set aside for about 5 minutes.
10. Carefully, scoop out the flesh, leaving about ¼-inch away from edges.
11. Drizzle the eggplant halves with one teaspoon of lemon juice.
12. Transfer the eggplant flesh into a bowl.
13. Add the tomatoes, salsa, parsley, salt, black pepper, remaining oil, and lemon juice and mix well.
14. Stuff the eggplant haves with salsa mixture and serve.

Nutrition:

Calories: 192, Carbohydrate: 33.8g, Protein: 6.9g, Fat: 6.1g, Sugar: 20.4g, Sodium: 204mg

Zucchini Salsa

Preparation Time: 20 minutes

Servings: 6

Ingredients:

- 1 ½ lb. zucchinis, roughly cubed
- 2 spring onions; chopped.
- 2 tomatoes; cubed
- 1 tbsp. balsamic vinegar
- Salt and black pepper to taste.

Directions:

1. In a pan that fits your air fryer, mix all the ingredients, toss, introduce the pan in the fryer and cook at 360 °F for 15 minutes
2. Divide the salsa into cups and serve cold.

Nutrition:

Calories: 164; Fat: 6g; Fiber: 2g; Carbs: 3g; Protein: 8g

Bacon Filled Poppers

Preparation Time: 5 minutes

Cooking Time: 15 minutes

Servings: 4

Ingredients:

- 4 strips crispy cooked bacon
- 3 tablespoons butter
- ½ cup jalapeno peppers, diced
- 2 oz. Cheddar cheese, white, shredded
- 2/3 cup almond flour
- 1 pinch cayenne pepper
- 1 tablespoon bacon fat
- 1 teaspoon kosher salt
- Black pepper, ground, to taste

Directions:

1. Preheat the Air fryer to 390 degrees F and grease an Air fryer basket.

2. Mix together butter with salt and water on medium heat in a skillet.
3. Whisk in the flour and sauté for about 3 minutes.
4. Dish out in a bowl and mix with the remaining ingredients to form a dough.
5. Wrap plastic wrap around the dough and refrigerate for about half an hour.
6. Make small popper balls out of this dough and arrange in the Air fryer basket.
7. Cook for about 15 minutes and dish out to serve warm.

Nutrition:

Calories: 385, Fat: 32.8g, Carbohydrates: 5.2g, Sugar: 0.4g, Protein: 17g, Sodium: 1532mg

Spiced Avocado Pudding

Preparation Time: 30 minutes

Servings: 6

Ingredients:

- 4 small avocados, peeled, pitted and mashed
- 1 cup coconut milk
- 2 eggs, whisked
- ¾ cup swerve
- 1 tsp. cinnamon powder
- ½ tsp. ginger powder

Directions:

1. Take a bowl and mix all the ingredients and whisk well.
2. Pour into a pudding mould, put it in the air fryer and cook at 350 °F for 25 minutes. Serve warm

Nutrition:

Calories: 192; Fat: 8g; Fiber: 2g; Carbs: 5g; Protein: 4g

Dried Raspberries

Preparation Time: 10 minutes

Cooking Time: 15 hours

Servings: 4

Ingredients:

- 4 cups raspberries, wash and dry
- 1/4 cup fresh lemon juice

Directions:

1. Add raspberries and lemon juice in a bowl and toss well.
2. Arrange raspberries on instant vortex air fryer oven tray and dehydrate at 135 °F for 12-15 hours.
3. Store in an air-tight container.

Nutrition:

Calories – 68 Protein – 1.6 g. Fat – 0.9 g. Carbs – 15 g.

Chocolate Strawberry Cups

Preparation Time: 15 minutes

Servings: 8

Ingredients:

- 16 strawberries; halved
- 2 cups chocolate chips; melted
- 2 tbsp. coconut oil

Directions:

1. In a pan that fits your air fryer, mix the strawberries with the oil and the melted chocolate chips, toss gently, put the pan in the air fryer and cook at 340 °F for 10 minutes.
2. Divide into cups and serve cold

Nutrition:

Calories: 162; Fat: 5g; Fiber: 3g; Carbs: 5g; Protein: 6g

Air Fryer Chocolate Cake

Preparation Time: 10 minutes

Cooking Time: 25 minutes

Servings: 6

Ingredients:

- 3 eggs
- 1 cup almond flour

- 1/3 cup cocoa powder
- 1 stick butter, room temperature
- 1½ teaspoons baking powder
- ½ cup sour cream
- 2/3 cup swerve
- 2 teaspoons vanilla

Directions:

1. Preheat the Air fryer to 360 degrees F and grease a cake pan lightly.
2. Mix all the ingredients in a bowl and beat well.
3. Pour the batter in the cake pan and transfer into the Air fryer basket.
4. Cook for about 25 minutes and cut into slices to serve.

Nutrition:

Calories: 313, Fats: 134g, Carbohydrates: 5.3g, Sugar: 19g, Proteins: 4.6g, Sodium: 62mg

Crème Brûlée

Preparation Time: 10 minutes

Cooking Time: 13 minutes

Servings: 8

Ingredients:
- 10 egg yolks
- 4 cups heavy cream

- 2 tablespoons vanilla extract
- 2 tablespoons sugar

Directions:

1. Preheat the Air fryer to 370 degrees F and grease 8: 6-ounce ramekins lightly.
2. Mix all the ingredients in a bowl except stevia until well combined.
3. Divide the mixture evenly in the ramekins and transfer into the Air fryer.
4. Cook for about 13 minutes and remove from the Air fryer.
5. Let it cool slightly and refrigerate for about 3 hours to serve.

Nutrition:

Calories: 295, Fat: 27.8g, Carbohydrates: 5.8g, Sugar: 3.6g, Protein: 4.6g, Sodium: 33mg

Zucchini-Choco Bread

Servings: 12

Cooking Time: 20 minutes

Ingredients

- ¼ teaspoon salt
- ½ cup maple syrup
- ½ cup almond milk

- 1 cup oat flour
- ½ cup sunflower oil
- ½ cup unsweetened cocoa powder
- 1 cup zucchini, shredded and squeezed
- 1 tablespoon flax egg: 1 tablespoon flax meal + 3 tablespoons water
- 1 teaspoon apple cider vinegar
- 1 teaspoon baking soda
- 1 teaspoon vanilla extract
- 1/3 cup chocolate chips

Directions:

1. Preheat the air fryer to 350 degrees F.
2. Line a baking dish that will fit the air fryer with parchment paper.
3. In a bowl, combine the flax meal, zucchini, sunflower oil, maple, vanilla, apple cider vinegar and milk.
4. Stir in the oat flour, baking soda, cocoa powder, and salt. Mix until well combined.

5. Add the chocolate chips.

6. Pour over the baking dish and cook for 15 minutes or until a toothpick inserted in the middle comes out clean.

Nutrition:

Calories: 213; Carbohydrates: 24.2 g; Protein: 4.6g; Fat: 10.9g

Yummy Banana Cookies

Servings: 6

Cooking Time: 10 minutes

Ingredients

- ripe bananas
- 1 teaspoon vanilla
- 1 cup dates, pitted and chopped

- 1/3 cup vegetable oil
- cups rolled oats

Directions:

1. Preheat the air fryer to 350 degrees F.
2. In a bowl, mash the bananas and add in the rest of the ingredients.
3. Let it rest inside the fridge for 10 minutes.
4. Drop a teaspoonful on cut parchment paper.
5. Place the cookies on parchment paper inside the air fryer basket. Make sure that the cookies do not overlap.
6. Cook for 20 minutes or until the edges are crispy.
7. Serve with almond milk.

Nutrition:

Calories: 382; Carbohydrates: 50.14g; Protein: 6.54g; Fat: 17.2g

Strawberry Muffins

Servings: 12

Preparation Time: 10 minutes

Cooking Time: 20 minutes

Ingredients:
- 3 eggs
- 1 tsp vanilla
- 2/3 cup strawberries, diced
- 1/3 cup heavy cream
- 1/2 cup Swerve
- 5 tbsp butter, melted
- 1 tsp cinnamon
- 2 tsp baking powder
- 2 ½ cups almond flour
- 1/4 tsp Himalayan salt

Directions
1. Preheat the air fryer to 176 C/ 350 F.
2. In a bowl, beat together butter and swerve. Add eggs, cream, and vanilla and beat until frothy.

3. Sift together almond flour, cinnamon, baking powder, and salt.
4. Add almond flour mixture to the wet ingredients and mix until well combined.
5. Add strawberries and stir well.
6. Pour batter into the muffin molds and place in air fryer. In batches.
7. Bake in for 20 minutes.
8. Serve and enjoy.

Nutrition Values:

Net Carbs: 3.6g; Calories: 208; Total Fat: 18.8g; Saturated Fat: 5g

Protein: 6.6g; Carbs: 6.4g

Notes

www.ingramcontent.com/pod-product-compliance
Lightning Source LLC
Chambersburg PA
CBHW070932080526
44589CB00013B/1482